P9-CML-283

WEST GA REG LIB SYS
Neva Lomason
Memorial Library
DISCARD

I WANT TO BE . . . BOOK SERIES
Creator/Producer: Stephanie Maze, Maze Productions
Writer and Educational Consultant: Catherine O'Neill Grace
Designer: Lisa Lytton-Smith

Photographers for I WANT TO BE AN ENGINEER:
Peter Menzel, Cary Wolinsky, Barbara Ries, Karen Kasmauski,
Paul Sancya, Nick Kelsh, Joanna Pinneo, Annie Griffiths Belt,
Richard T. Nowitz, Joe McNally, Joel Sartore, Steve Ringman,
Lara Jo Regan, Bill Tiernan, J. Kyle Keener

Other books in this series:
I WANT TO BE AN ASTRONAUT
I WANT TO BE A DANCER
I WANT TO BE A VETERINARIAN

Copyright © 1997 by Maze Productions
Photography credits appear on page 48.

All rights reserved. No part of this publication may be reproduced or
transmitted in any form or by any means, electronic or mechanical,
including photocopy, recording, or any information storage and retrieval
system, without permission in writing from the publisher.

Requests for permission to make copies
of any part of the work should be mailed to:
Permissions Department, Harcourt Brace & Company,
6277 Sea Harbor Drive, Orlando, Florida 32887-6777.

Library of Congress Cataloging-in-Publication Data
Maze, Stephanie.
I want to be an engineer/by Stephanie Maze and Catherine O'Neill Grace.
p. cm.—(I want to be . . . book series)
Summary: Describes the work of the various branches of engineering.
ISBN 0-15-201298-2
1. Engineering—Vocational guidance—Juvenile literature. 2. Engineers—
Vocational guidance—Juvenile Literature.
[1. Engineers. 2. Occupations.] I. Grace, Catherine O'Neill, 1950–
II. Title. III. Series.
TA157.M3415 1997
620'.0023—dc20 96-26982

First edition
A C E F D B

Pre-press through PrintNet
Printed and bound by Tien Wah Press, Singapore

I Want to Be...

AN ENGINEER

A Maze Productions Book

HARCOURT BRACE & COMPANY

SAN DIEGO   NEW YORK   LONDON

ACKNOWLEDGMENTS

We wish to thank the following people, companies, and institutions for their very valuable contributions to this book: Henry Petroski, Chair, Department of Civil and Environmental Engineering, Duke University; Jeffrey Leaf, Thomas Jefferson High School for Science and Technology; Mary Paris, Director of Communications, National Society of Professional Engineers; Dan Kunz, Executive Director, Junior Engineering Technical Society (JETS); Greg Pearson, Editor, National Academy of Engineering; Dr. Jay Jaroslav, Research Scientist and Director, Office of Strategic Planning, Artificial Intelligence Laboratory, Massachusetts Institute of Technology; Don L. Everton Jr., Vice President, Norshipco; Anne Perusek, Editor, SWE Magazine; Dawsalee Griffin, The Boeing Company; Janet Staats, Du Pont Company; Ken Vogel, Metropolitan Washington Airports Authority; Kristin Kinley, Ford Motor Company; Darian Germain, Sprint; Nagisa Yamamoto, Industrial Light & Magic; Alana Rothstein, Amalgamated Dynamics, Inc.; Society of Women Engineers; Eric Delony, Historic American Engineering Record; Chuck Blue, National Academy of Engineering; Stephen A. Gates, American Society of Civil Engineers; Mark Monjeau, Project Create; Purdue University; Massachusetts Institute of Technology; George Washington University; Occidental College; Mike Gentry, NASA Media Resource Center, Houston; Dia Stolnitz, U.S. FIRST, The Competition; American Vocational Association; Rick Smolan; Thomas K. Walker, Graf-x, New York; A & I Color Laboratory, Los Angeles.

Many thanks, also, to the very talented people who have participated in the I WANT TO BE . . . project: the photographers, writer Catherine O'Neill Grace, and designer Lisa Lytton-Smith, as well as our colleagues at Harcourt Brace Children's Books, publisher Louise Howton Pelan and editor Karen Weller-Watson, whose guidance has been invaluable.

And finally, our heartfelt gratitude to all the professionals in this book for allowing us to interrupt their busy schedules and for agreeing to be the wonderful role models children can look up to for many years to come.

To all children who dream the impossible dreams

Where to Start

Are you reading this book by the glow of an electric light? The generators, power lines, and circuits that brought the energy into your house to light the bulb were invented, designed, and built by engineers. Do you take a bus to school, carpool, ride your bike, or walk? The design of your bike, the roadway system you travel on, the safety belt or helmet that could save your life in a crash were all developed by engineers. If you log on to a computer when you get to school, you can thank engineers again for designing the hardware and software.

If you like to build things, solve problems, and make systems work better, you could be an engineer. You need to develop your math skills, communication skills, and knowledge of science and logic so that you can work effectively on teams with other problem solvers.

Engineers turn ideas into reality. They solve practical problems with science and technology. Part scientist, part technician, part inventor, an engineer designs and produces things—from roadways to roller coasters, jet engines to juicers, and cars to computer chips.

Computers are central to engineering today. In the picture at right, mechanical engineer Kem D. Alhers uses a computer "virtual reality" system that simulates a test track to check the steering of a huge earthmoving machine called a Caterpillar. The system is located at the National Center for Supercomputing Applications in Champaign, Illinois. Using it, Alhers can maneuver and simulate scooping up gravel while hearing lifelike sounds.

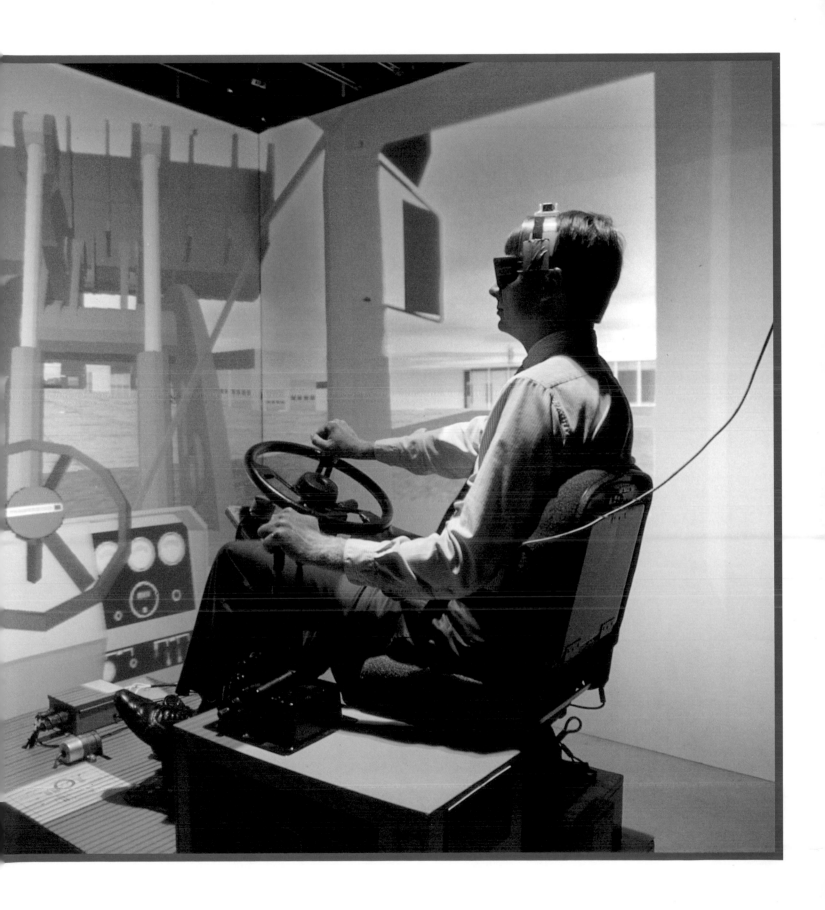

Construction Engineer

Code Engineer

Engineers indoors and out. These experts are all hard at work on the same project: building a new terminal at National Airport, near Washington, D.C. Victoria Hankerson reviews plans near the structure (top left). Ray Lum measures a blueprint (top right).

Structural engineer Roderick Hosang checks cables that will be used in constructing the terminal (left). On the site, Gilbert E. Jones keeps in touch with workers (below left). Inside the new terminal, Larry Chandler checks electrical switches and circuits (below).

Safety Engineer

Electrical Engineer

8

Types of Engineers

Agricultural Engineer

Mechanical Engineer

Environmental Engineer

Engineers work on many kinds of problems. At Purdue University in West Lafayette, Indiana, Dirk E. Maier, a professor of biochemical and food processing engineering, analyzes cereal quality (above left). Mechanical and industrial engineer Pete Worth examines pipes in a boiler room that will heat a new terminal building at National Airport near Washington, D.C. (above center). Environmental engineer Mario Vasquez checks water quality at a Du Pont waste treatment plant, where water is cleaned before it flows back into the Delaware River (above right).

Our complex industrial world depends on an amazing array of machines and systems to provide food, water, shelter, and energy; to move people from place to place; and to make instant communication possible. Not only do engineers develop these systems, they keep them running and work to make them better. There are several broad categories of engineers to do all these jobs and many specialists within each category.

Mechanical engineers develop new machinery and adapt old systems for new uses. They make people comfortable by inventing more efficient heating and cooling systems, and they plan ways to make manufacturing processes operate smoothly and safely.

Civil engineers design transportation systems, irrigation systems, and water treatment plants.

They design, build, and maintain bridges and roads. They figure out how to keep airplanes moving safely through the complex air-traffic control system. They may even design amusement park rides.

Electrical engineers design systems and equipment to generate and deliver electricity, including huge dams and tiny computer circuits. They work in electronics, too—on lasers, stereo systems, robots, computers, and worldwide communication networks. They also figure out how to communicate with spacecraft.

Chemical engineers use their knowledge and imagination to invent useful combinations of chemical substances and to synthesize new materials. They devise systems to control pollution, and they work on creating stronger plastics. They also join physicians in their efforts to develop drugs to combat AIDS, cancer, and other illnesses.

Within these broad categories there are many, many specialties. The specialists include automotive engineers, who design and build cars, and aerospace engineers, who work on spacecraft. Biotechnology engineers use living things such as bacteria or genes to make or change products and to treat illnesses. Ceramics engineers find methods for transforming sand and clay into products such as computer chips and unbreakable glass.

Construction engineers develop ways to make buildings tall and functional as well as energy efficient and resistant to natural forces such as earthquakes and hurricanes. Environmental engineers devise production methods that pollute the environment as little as possible, and they find ways to clean up the messes that outdated manufacturing and transportation systems leave behind. Fire protection engineers develop methods to fight fires more successfully. Naval engineers design ships. Plastics engineers make stronger, lighter materials and work to improve recycling.

Engineers will be important shapers of the world in the twenty-first century. Do you want to get involved?

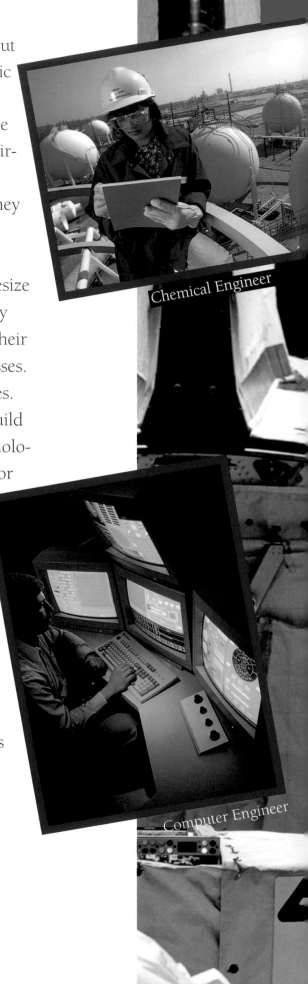

Chemical Engineer

Computer Engineer

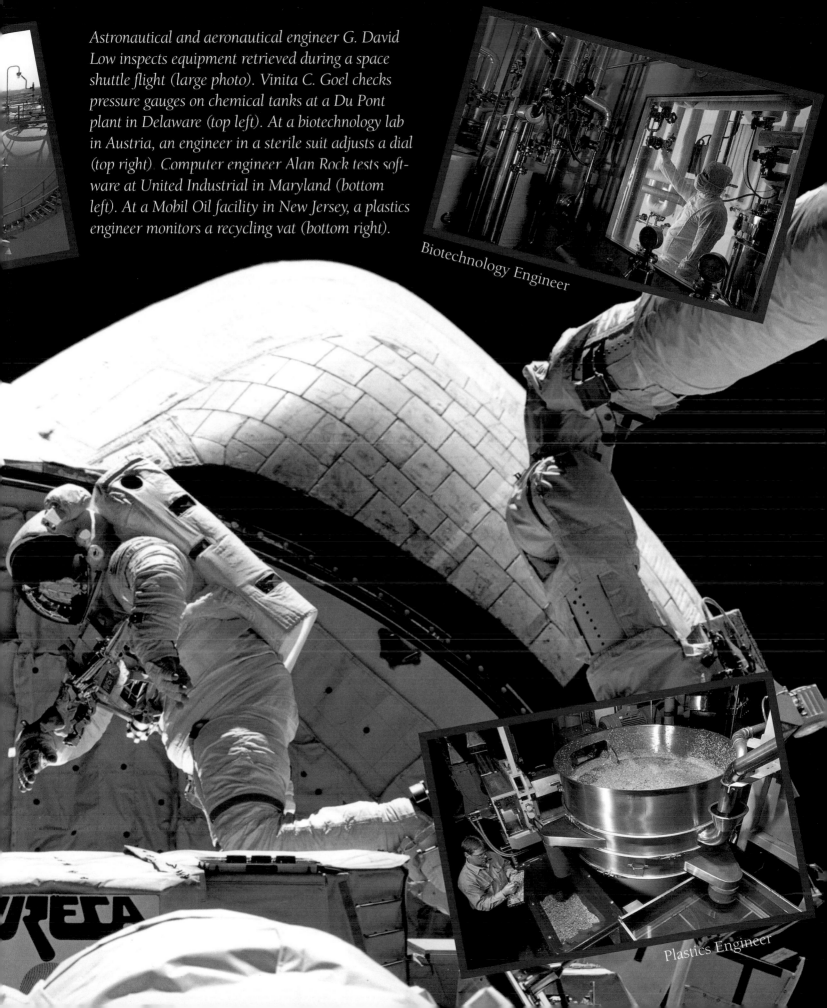

Astronautical and aeronautical engineer G. David Low inspects equipment retrieved during a space shuttle flight (large photo). Vinita C. Goel checks pressure gauges on chemical tanks at a Du Pont plant in Delaware (top left). At a biotechnology lab in Austria, an engineer in a sterile suit adjusts a dial (top right). Computer engineer Alan Rock tests software at United Industrial in Maryland (bottom left). At a Mobil Oil facility in New Jersey, a plastics engineer monitors a recycling vat (bottom right).

Biotechnology Engineer

Plastics Engineer

EURECA

Engineering a Car

The Ford Mustang has been a dream car for millions of motorists since it was first introduced in 1964. An automobile that sported the logo of a galloping pony—a symbol of freedom and excitement (above)—the Mustang almost instantly became one of the top five automobiles in the United States. During the first four months that it was available, it had a hundred thousand buyers! The Ford Motor Company engineers had worked hard at the Dearborn, Michigan, headquarters to create the car, and they had a lot to celebrate. Then they went right back to their plans, models, and test laboratories to work on making the Mustang more powerful, more efficient, and safer.

Engineers have been involved in every step of Mustang production—from design to manufacturing and safety testing. Improvements on the Mustang continue today with the help of high-tech equipment that car designers in the 1960s didn't dream of. Above, product design engineer Lisa Cratty and designer Paul Arnone work at a paintbox computer as they dream up a Ford Mustang for the twenty-first century.

Thomas Jefferson High School for Science and Technology in Fairfax, Virginia, has many well-equipped laboratories, where students study disciplines such as computer-aided design, microelectronics, and biotechnology. "TJ" students are also paired with mentors who are technology professionals in industry and universities. Teacher Jeffrey Leaf (above left in tie) helps some students in a mechanical engineering class explore the electronic components of everyday objects— including a sewing machine—while other students take apart a VCR (above right).

Or you might consider a co-op program that lets you work as a technician in an engineering profession while earning your degree.

Engineers use their knowledge of math, science, and technology to solve problems and to create new systems or machinery. They plan and design projects from concept to completion. This process involves making calculations and drafting plans.

Today pursuing any scientific or technical career—but especially engineering—means understanding and being comfortable with computers and computer programming. Engineering study includes working on computers to create statistical and mathematical models of new ideas. Engineers-in-training also use computer-aided design (CAD) to draft blueprints of equipment they want to build or to create flow charts of projects they want to do. But it isn't enough just to have a great blueprint of an idea on a computer printout; engineers have to be able to build things, too. And the things they build have to work!

To develop the technical skills they need, engineering students learn by doing. Above far left, many hands organize electrical wires at the Electronic Data Systems Internship Program for Chantilly High School students in Chantilly, Virginia. Above center, students in a two-year engineering program at Northern Virginia Community College in Annandale, Virginia, work on a circuit board under the guidance of professor Rassa Rassai. Above right, Stephanie LaRue of Purdue University in Indiana machines parts for a car. These students' hands-on experiences give them the mechanical skills they need to turn their ideas into reality.

Putting it together. At right, Massachusetts Institute of Technology student Jerry Pratt works on a robot called Spring Turkey in the Artificial Intelligence Lab in Cambridge, Massachusetts. The robot simulates the way a bird walks. Below, student Michael Hobson works on a "mini-baja," a land/water vehicle. Hobson is enrolled in the mechanical engineering department at Purdue University in West Lafayette, Indiana.

Competitions

Each year inventive engineers in elementary schools, middle schools, high schools, and colleges enter a variety of technology competitions and fairs. The young people who entered the engineering contests shown on these pages have discovered something important about engineering: It's creative and it's fun!

Some of the contests are pretty wacky, like the National Rube Goldberg™ Machine Contest, named for a cartoonist who drew weird, incredibly complicated contraptions that performed simple tasks. In 1996 the task set by the Rube Goldberg™ competition, held each year at Purdue University in West Lafayette, Indiana, was to get a coin into a bank—in no *fewer* than twenty steps! Students from the University of Wisconsin didn't win the 1996 contest, but they had a great time building a machine they called Money Grubbers (bottom).

In the large photo (facing page), radio-controlled "robo-gladiators" built by high school students fight during a U.S. FIRST robotic competition in New Hampshire. The brainchild of engineer Dean Kamen, the contest is a national elimination tournament that calls on kids' inventive and engineering skills as well as their desire to win. Kamen hopes that the U.S. FIRST contest will be featured on TV someday—like the Superbowl or the World Series—and will inspire kids everywhere to create useful inventions.

Building the future. *Elementary school participants in Project Create (top) showcase underwater communities at a fair in Orlando, Florida. The Future City Competition™, which is part of National Engineers Week every year throughout the United States, has students use a computer game to design an energy-efficient city and then build a three-dimensional model of it (above center).*

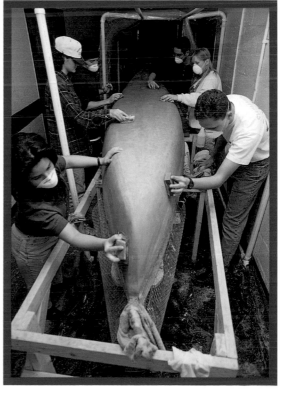

College contests. *Engineering students at Purdue University perform last-minute checks on their solar car before a race in Australia (above). At George Washington University in Washington, D.C., students smooth out the rough edges of their canoe before entering it in a national concrete canoe competition (right).*

The History of Engineering

Engineering is a profession that contributes to making life better for large numbers of people. For example, Roman engineers built aqueducts to carry clean water from faraway hills into the city. Beginning around 300 B.C. and continuing for five centuries, the results were an eight-hundred-mile system, some of which ran on top of multileveled, arched bridges like the one in the photo at top right. Part of civilized life for ancient Romans was enjoying outdoor baths—thanks to engineers.

The Roman engineers were not the first inventive people to design structures for carrying water into human settlements. Simple aqueducts had been devised in the Middle East even earlier. But Romans are considered the first civil engineers. They built extensive systems of bridges and roads to move their armies and enlarge their empire.

Engineers build systems to carry water, ease travel, and house people. From putting up the first huts to erecting the highest skyscrapers, they have built shelters and workplaces. The structure may be a cozy house or a beautiful place in which to practice religion. In medieval Europe, engineers found ways to make cathedrals structurally sound *and* beautiful, like Notre-Dame de Paris, in France (center). Built during the late twelfth and early thirteenth centuries, Notre Dame has pointed Gothic arches, which are very strong. It also has structural supports called flying buttresses—

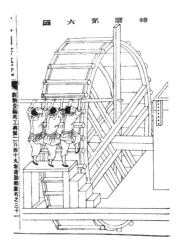

Marvels of engineering. *Through the centuries engineers have used building materials and their own ingenuity to move water through aqueducts (top), build houses of worship (center), and harness the energy of wind power (above left) and human muscle (above right).*

TREVITHICKS,
PORTABLE STEAM ENGINE.

Catch me who can.

Mechanical Power Subduing
Animal Speed.

*Famous engineers.
James Watt (above) perfected the steam engine.
America's first president,
George Washington
(left), called for engineering schools. Inventor
Eli Whitney (below)
created machinery with
interchangeable parts.*

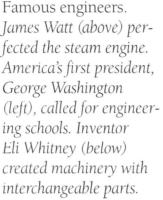

GUNSMITH

the curved projections at the back of the building. The design of the buttresses allowed cathedral builders to put up taller, thinner walls adorned with stained-glass windows.

Through the centuries engineers have invented tools, put up buildings, bridged rivers, and tunneled through rock. They have harnessed the energy of wind using windmills (facing page, bottom left), and they have devised machinery that harnesses human energy, such as the Chinese treadwheel detailed in an eighteenth-century woodcut (facing page, bottom right). Similar wheels using moving water, instead of people, are still in use at mills around the world.

Beginning in the 1700s engineers began to figure out ways to use the energy in the steam released by boiling water. They developed engines that converted steam energy into mechanical energy. James Watt, a Scotsman, is often credited with inventing the steam engine. But his real accomplishment—one that changed the world—was perfecting the design of the engine so that it could use steam power effectively. This new steam technology led to the design and manufacturing of self-powered engines such as coal carts that moved on tracks in the mines (bottom).

Historians often cite the development of the steam engine as the start of a period in modern history called the industrial revolution. This revolution, which began in England but quickly spread to Europe and America, transformed the way people worked and how they got from place to place. A major contributor to this change was

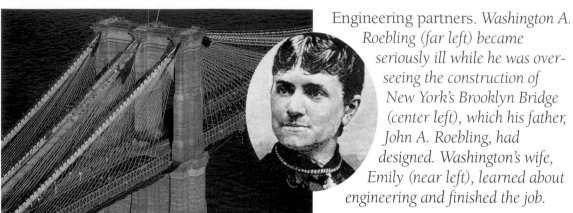

Engineering partners. *Washington A. Roebling (far left) became seriously ill while he was overseeing the construction of New York's Brooklyn Bridge (center left), which his father, John A. Roebling, had designed. Washington's wife, Emily (near left), learned about engineering and finished the job.*

the steam locomotive, introduced by Richard Trevithick. In 1804 Trevithick applied Watt's steam technology to transportation. The first U.S. railway train ran in 1825, and this new-fangled way to get from place to place caught on fast. By 1869 a transcontinental railway line stretched across the United States, all the way from the Atlantic to the Pacific.

This period of rapid technological change created a need to formally educate engineers. The first engineering school opened in Paris in 1794. Several years later President George Washington called for the creation of an engineering school in the United States. In 1824 the first civilian U.S. engineering school, Rensselaer Polytechnic Institute, opened its doors in Troy, New York.

With the development of steam power and new transportation systems, innovative ways to build and manufacture things were also implemented. In the United States an inventor named Eli Whitney came up with the idea of parts that could be used in making many different products. Eventually, interchangeable parts would lead to mass production of everything from automobiles to weapons.

Assembly line. *Henry Ford's economical manufacturing methods (above) allowed him to lower prices. A Ford cost $780 in 1910. By 1924 the price had dropped to $290. At that price, even people with modest incomes could buy one.*

Important innovators. *George Westinghouse (near right) founded the company that bears his name and was one of the first engineers to use the assembly line (center right). He's famous for harnessing the energy of electricity. Thomas Edison (far right) invented the lightbulb— and hundreds of other useful devices.*

Forms of communication were changing, too. Samuel Morse (facing page, second row, right) invented the telegraph in 1837, making it possible to send long-distance messages rapidly. Huge steamships, including the *Great Eastern* (facing page, second row, left), laid an undersea cable from Europe to America in 1866.

Engineers have been busy in the twentieth century, too. During the 1900s Henry Ford (facing page, bottom) combined various technologies in a way that changed the world. He used interchangeable parts, and he devised a mechanical system of conveyor belts to move his product, an automobile, through a factory assembly line. Using this method, Ford could make many more cars than his competition could. The result: the affordable Model T. Introduced in 1908, the Model T Ford was the first car that working-class people were able to buy.

Cars, trains, rapid communication. Sounds a lot like the world we live in, doesn't it? But there were some major differences—no television, for one. Engineer Vladimir Zworykin (right) is holding a device that changed that. The 1929 version of the cathode ray tube on his lap eventually evolved into the television screen.

Going up. *You wouldn't easily get to the top of the 1,454-foot Sears Tower in Chicago (above), or of any skyscraper, without an elevator. Elevator design is still based on the 1850s invention of Elisha Otis and the pulley that lowered and raised the elevator (inset above).*

Great Feats of the Twentieth Century

Technology builds on technology—so new inventions often lead to new products and record-breaking achievements. Can you think of other engineering wonders that exist today?

GOLDEN GATE BRIDGE
1937

TELEVISION
1931

APOLLO MOON LANDING
1969

PANAMA CANAL
1914

APPLICATION SATELLITES
1957

ARTIFICIAL HEART
1967

AIRCRAFT CARRIER
1958

TRANS-ALASKA PIPELINE
1977

NUCLEAR POWER
1950s

FIBER-OPTIC COMMUNICATIONS
1977

COMBINE HARVESTER
1975

GENETIC ALTERATIONS
1981

EMPIRE STATE BUILDING
1931

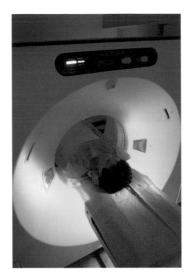
CAT SCAN
1970s

MICROPROCESSOR
1958

JUMBO JETS
1969

COMPOSITE MATERIALS
1985

AQUA-LUNG ™
1943

LASERS
1956

COMPUTER-AIDED DESIGN
1970s

SYDNEY OPERA HOUSE
1973

BULLET TRAINS
1971

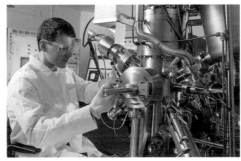
ELECTRON MICROSCOPE
1931

SYNTHETIC FIBER
1930s

Did You Know . . .

. . . that at 630 feet, the Gateway Arch in St. Louis, Missouri, is the tallest monument in the United States? The stainless steel arch frames downtown St. Louis. Built in 1965, the Gateway Arch is a tribute to the thousands of nineteenth-century pioneers who headed west from this spot.

. . . that lasers can cut through concrete or steel? Other uses for lasers—beams of pure light—include drilling eyes in needles, measuring distance with precision, and performing delicate eye and brain surgery.

. . . that Leonardo da Vinci, an Italian artist and inventor who lived from 1452–1519, designed a flying machine that might have worked except that the power source to get it aloft hadn't been invented yet? He also drew pictures of ideas for an arched bridge, a parachute, and a bicycle—all of which would be reinvented centuries later.

. . . that the circuit on a half-inch-square silicon chip in a computer may contain several million parts?

. . . that the technology for freezing food was developed in the 1950s, revolutionizing farming and the way people prepare meals?

. . . that the longest roadway tunnel in the world is in Switzerland? The St. Gotthard Tunnel burrows 10.1 miles through the rock of the Alps.

. . . that the zipper was invented by Whitcomb L. Judson in the United States in 1893? He came up with the idea because people complained about how long it took to put on or take off buttoned shoes and boots.

. . . that the huge machines that bored through earth and rock to create the Chunnel, the underwater Channel Tunnel between England and France, weighed thirteen hundred tons each?

. . . that stainless steel, an important building material, was first made by accident? Engineers have discovered many things by making mistakes as they develop a product. You might say that making mistakes is part of the engineering process!

. . . that the Sony Corporation was issued the patent for the first portable cassette player—the Walkman—in 1981?

Engineering Vocabulary

Engineering is a highly technical profession. It has many specialized branches, from agriculture to sound engineering, building design to computer work, robotics to power generation. On these two pages are some of the words engineers use to describe their tools, processes, and inventions.

GENERATORS

Inside power stations such as this, generators convert mechanical energy into electric current. The mechanical energy can derive from sources including a hydroelectric dam, or steam generated by heat from burning coal, oil, or gas, or from nuclear energy. Power-station generators feed electricity into cables and wires that supply homes and businesses.

BLUEPRINTS

Blueprints are drawn and written plans for projects that engineers design, from skyscrapers to microcomputer circuits. Long ago, blueprints were created by draftsmen who worked with pen and paper. Today blueprints are likely to be created on computers. At every stage in a project, engineers consult blueprints to make sure they are following the steps of a project correctly.

CIRCUIT BOARD

Electrical components are often attached to a flat sheet known as a circuit board, like the one being put together here. On the board, electricity passes through each circuit, or loop, of conducting material through which electrons can flow easily. An electric appliance contains many circuits, in a variety of shapes, sizes, and materials. These parts are called components.

SEMICONDUCTOR

Semiconductors are materials that conduct electricity but allow easy control of the flow of current. Silicon, a common element found in sand and other minerals, is probably the best-known semiconductor. Computer chips—which are like miniaturized circuit boards with thousands upon thousands of components on them—are made from silicon.

SOLAR PANELS

The sun radiates huge amounts of energy. Solar panels capture this energy and the solar cells that cover the panels are capable of converting sunlight directly into electricity. In sunny places, people install solar panels on their homes to generate electricity. Out in space, solar panels are used to generate power for spacecraft.

FIBER OPTICS

Developed for the telephone industry, fiber-optics technology transmits information such as Internet messages through glass threads thinner than a human hair. Waves of light are used to move coded pulses through the fibers. Fiber optics has other uses, including threading light into the human body during delicate surgery.

TURBINE ENGINE

A turbine engine consists of blades attached to a central shaft. When a current such as moving water or steam passes over the blade, the turbine spins. The rotating shaft can be used to operate other machinery or to generate electricity. The earliest form of turbine engine was the waterwheel, which has been in use for centuries.

DIESEL ENGINE

The diesel engine is the most efficient kind of internal combustion engine. It is high performance, heavy, and thick walled. Diesel engines—like this one being serviced on a ship at the Norshipco yard in Norfolk, Virginia—are most often used to power large vehicles like ships, trucks, buses, and locomotives.

LASER DISC

Information in the form of sound, pictures, and data are stored on the shiny surface of a laser disc. Areas where information is recorded turn dull. To retrieve information, a laser beam is directed at the disc as it spins. The beam reflects off the dull and shiny surface into a detector, which decodes the flashes.

ROBOTIC ARM

Manufacturing involves many tasks that are too dangerous, or too repetitive, for people to do by hand; the solution: a robotic arm. Mechanical arms don't get tired or bored. They can handle toxic materials and withstand very hot, cold, or toxic environments. Most factory robots consist of "arms" like these.

Technology at Work

Engineers get the job done! The photos on these pages show people with whom engineers work every day, such as technicians, physicians, research chemists, and construction workers. Some work with lasers to take precise measurements as they build machinery (large photo, facing page). Others work with chemical products such as oil to make them less threatening to the environment (bottom). Some interact with other people—including babies (bottom left, facing page). Still others work with art objects such as paintings and old statues (bottom right, facing page). Engineering presents a lot of possibilities!

One of the most important tasks of engineering in the late twentieth century is finding ways to clean up pollution caused by manufacturing processes and human consumption and waste. This can involve harnessing natural processes to help out. Scott Sargert (top) manages an experimental greenhouse in Providence, Rhode Island. He is comparing sewer water before and after it has been treated with natural methods for breaking down pollutants. (The "before" vial is in his left hand.) The water is pumped into the vats behind him, where plants, bacteria, snails, and fish naturally consume, digest, filter, or break down the pollution to convert sewage into clean water. After five days in the vats, the water is safe to discharge back into rivers— and it even *smells* good.

At the Smith-Kettlewell Eye Research

Institute in San Francisco, California, Dr. Anthony M. Norcia records a seven-week-old baby's responses to images flashed on a computer screen while his associate, Russell D. Hamer, looks on (bottom left, facing page).

Dr. Norcia is interested in figuring out what babies see. The system he uses—designed and fabricated by engineers—measures the baby's brain responses to certain images. Results of this research suggest that a baby's visual system develops earlier than people used to believe it did.

Engineers and their colleagues also restore, repair, and rebuild things. Restoration of the Statue of Liberty, in preparation for her one hundredth birthday in 1986, involved many engineers and technicians. To get metal restoration experts all the way up to the statue's face, the world's tallest freestanding scaffold had to be erected—and then disassembled. It was gigantic because it had to cover both the 150-foot pedestal *and* the 152-foot Lady Liberty.

Engineering technicians repair computers to keep information moving (top). To keep cars moving, workers solder parts of an overpass near Houston, Texas (second from top). Aerospace engineers work on the engines that power the space shuttle (second from bottom).

Engineers often work in teams, like the Motorola computer experts (bottom) collaborating on new ways to make computer chips store more information. These electronics specialists are working on a blown-up blueprint of a chip that monitors pressure inside car engines. Modern design and manufacturing projects often involve so many different team members that there's a whole branch of engineering, called systems engineering, that trains people to track projects and to keep them running smoothly.

Wearing safety goggles to protect her eyes, a chemist works at a New York biotechnology production facility (top). She monitors elaborate equipment that produces chemicals through fermentation, a process in which bacteria change natural substances into chemicals. The chemicals produced will be used to manufacture medicines, such as antibiotics to cure infections. Chemical researchers must understand biology and chemistry, and they must be able to work with complicated machinery like the pressurized vats in this photograph.

At Escagen, a biotechnology company, a biotechnologist tests disease-free potato seeds (bottom left). The seeds will save farmers lots of money because fewer of these seeds are needed to plant a successful crop. A pilot (bottom right) "flies" in a cockpit simulator designed by computer and aeronautics engineers. Practicing with this equipment presents him with real-life flying situations, including emergencies. It gives the pilot hours of danger-free experience at the controls.

Movie Magic

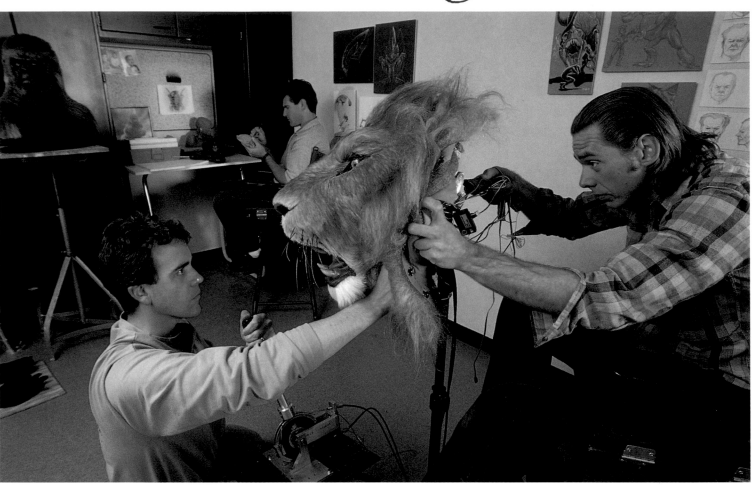

Engineers who work in the movie business can picture amazing things in their heads and make them happen on screen. But there are a lot of steps between imagination and what you actually see in a movie theater. Let's go behind the scenes to see motion picture engineers at work.

Jumanji is the story of two kids who play a magic board game that makes animals such as lions and rhinos come dramatically to life right inside their house. Many of the amazing animatronic special effects in the movie were the work of Amalgamated Dynamics, Inc. (ADI), of Los Angeles, California. Animatronics is the science of engineering models that move following the commands of built-in electronic programs. Above, ADI director Tom Woodruff and engineer George Bernota are working on the circuits that will bring a lion's head roaring to life. In the background, Alec Gillis, ADI's other director, checks some of the wiring. Those are George Bernota's hands fiddling in the "guts" of an animatronic spider in the small photo at left.

The creatures in *Jumanji* were both anima-

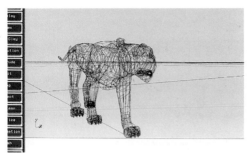

Bringing a lion to life. On his screen, Industrial Light & Magic computer wizard Carl Frederick combines the pieces that create an animated lion for the movie Jumanji (above). At right are four digital shot breakdowns that together create a scene of the lion strolling in a hallway (from the top): the empty hallway; a "wire-frame" model created with the computer to show how the image will take up space; the wire-frame placed on top of the hallway image; and the drawn-in lion come to life.

tronic models and digital animated drawings that were created by another company, Industrial Light & Magic (ILM), in San Rafael, California. ILM is world-famous for its state-of-the-art computerized special effects. ILM designers have won dozens of Academy Awards for Best Visual Effects and Technical Achievement. Above, ILM computer graphics supervisor Carl Frederick works at his terminal, combining the different parts of an animated scene. You might think that Carl Frederick's education was in art and film. In fact, he studied mathematics and computers. He's a computer engineer!

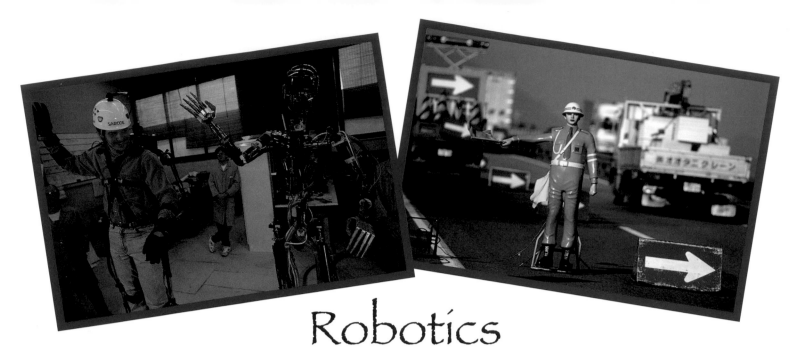

Robotics

Have you ever wanted a robot to help you out with the tasks of daily life? You may not have a personal robot helper yet, but robots already play a major role in manufacturing things you use at home. In Japan a robot traffic cop helps keep vehicles moving safely (top right). The Japanese name for the robot is *anzen taro,* or "traffic boy." Another Japanese robot serves the Oobuchi family at the Grazie Italian restaurant in Tokyo (bottom left). The waiter robot, named Ken-Chan, is engineered to speak as well as serve; its phrases include "Welcome" and "You all look happy." Robots of the future will take the place of people in doing dangerous jobs, including fire fighting. In Utah a firefighter demonstrates body positions as an engineer works on a robot that imitates human motion (top left). Robots may also take the place of workers in fields such as construction. In the photo below (bottom right), a civil engineer works on designing software that will allow robots to build walls, then paint them.

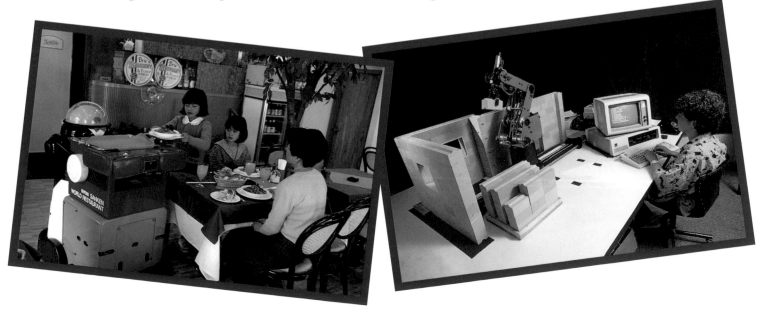

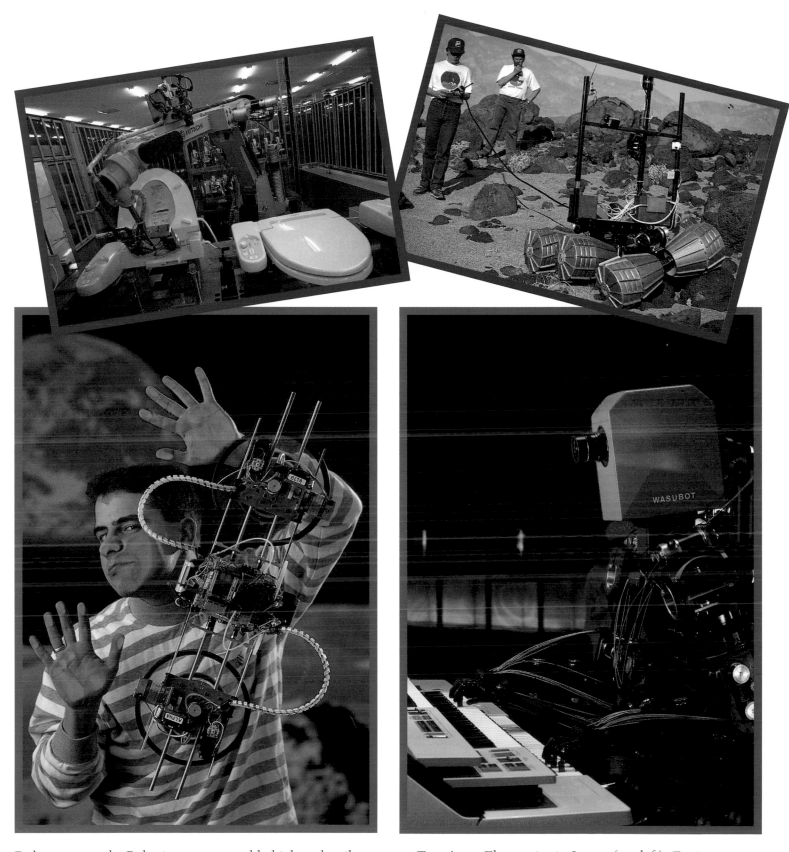

Robots at work. *Robotic arms assemble high-tech toilet seats at Toto Aqua Electronics in Japan (top left). Engineers test the Mars Rover, which will be used to explore the red planet's surface, in the rugged terrain of Death Valley (top right). A glass panel separates Massachusetts Institute of Technology student Chris Foley from Eddie, the wall-climbing, suction-footed robot he designed in the MIT Artificial Intelligence Laboratory (above left). A robot reads music and plays piano at a science expo in Japan (above right).*

High Tech

The new equipment, techniques, and communication systems such as the Internet that engineers design change lives for the better. At left, a patient undergoes laser eye surgery. Using the thin, concentrated beams of light, surgeons can repair eye injuries such as detached retinas with amazing precision.

In the top photo, a technician uses bar codes like the ones scanned in your grocery store to track samples of human DNA (deoxyribonucleic acid). The black bars and white spaces on bar codes are read by a beam of infrared light from the device the technician holds. DNA, a substance found in human tissue, carries genetic information. Every human has unique DNA. It can be used in many ways, from medical research to analyzing evidence in crime cases.

You might not think that playing with Legos™ could lead to a career in engineering. But why not? Building with the toy blocks, you use design and problem-solving skills, the ability to imagine in three dimensions, and patience. Now meet Dr. LegoHead. Developed By Rick Borovoy (center) at the MIT Media Laboratory, a place for research about new information technology, the "intelligent" toy allows kids to use electronics to make it move and talk.

On-line. *At Sprint's Network Management Center in Reston, Virginia (above), communications experts work at banks of terminals as they monitor Internet transmissions and flow of data for private companies. If you "surf" through the information on the World Wide Web, chances are these people are helping. Sprint is the largest Internet access provider in the world.*

In a grain of sand. *Silicon (above left), the basic ingredient in sand, is used to make computer chips such as in the "clean room" in Research Triangle Park, North Carolina (above right). At the University of Haifa in Israel, a technician works on installing microelectronics components in an automated artificial hand (top). Krista Caudill, who is deaf and blind, tests a finger-spelling robotic hand at the Alfred I. duPont Institute in Wilmington, Delaware (above center).*

International Engineering

Throughout the world, engineers work to build new structures, improve the quality of life, and solve problems caused by pollution or age. The Tower of Pisa (left), completed six centuries ago, has long been nicknamed the Leaning Tower. Over time it tilted seventeen feet out of vertical as the soft ground beneath it settled unevenly. This tower in northern Italy has been restored by engineers to keep it from tilting further.

High tech is worldwide. In Hong Kong a technician checks the quality of semiconductors (top right). Beneath the English Channel, earth and rocks are removed during the excavation of the Channel Tunnel, nicknamed the Chunnel (second from top, right). Now in daily use, the thirty-one-mile-long tunnel has a twenty-four-mile underwater section, the world's longest.

Technology also has worldwide side effects. When coal and oil are burned to provide power for manufacturing, chemicals are released that combine with water in clouds to produce acid rain. Acid rain damages crops, buildings, and monuments. A restoration specialist in Venice, Italy, cleans a statue harmed by acid rain (second from bottom, right).

In China a huge new dam will displace millions of people from their homes. Some experts say the dam is needed to control the Yangtze River's flooding, but the financial and human cost is very high. Technology can also be helpful, however. At the International Rice Research Institute in the Philippines, a genetic engineer works to develop a kind of rice that can be grown easily to feed hungry people (bottom right).

Engineers work at Carajás Mine in Brazil, the largest iron-ore mine in the world (above). Construction workers crowd the site of the Yangtze River Dam in China (right). The dam will be the world's largest. A reservoir will flood land behind the dam, forcing a million people to move.

Some Noteworthy Engineers

Sometimes engineers' names are linked with inventions—like James Watt's with the steam engine. Other engineers remain anonymous because they solve problems as part of a team. Others may be well-known in their fields but unfamiliar to nonengineers. Here are some important engineers.

BENJAMIN WRIGHT
Called the father of civil engineering, Wright, who lived from 1770–1842, was chief engineer of the Erie Canal, which made travel and trade possible from Lake Erie to the Hudson River.

THOMAS TELFORD
This Scottish engineer built the world's first suspension bridge in Wales, completed in 1826. Telford also created elevated roads for better drainage and covered them with large paving stones.

SYLVANUS THAYER
Thayer pioneered engineering education in America by adapting French educational practices to such new schools as Thayer School of Civil Engineering, which he founded at Dartmouth College.

CHARLES STARK DRAPER
Known as Doc, Draper was the inventor of modern navigation systems. He developed practical systems for long-distance navigation for aircraft, space vehicles, strategic missiles, and submarines.

LILLIAN M. GILBRETH
Collaborating with her husband, Gilbreth worked on time-and-motion studies designed to help companies become more efficient. This industrial engineer also raised twelve children.

MARIO MOLINA
The first Latino Nobel Prize winner for chemistry, in 1995, chemical engineer Molina was the first scientist to suggest that man-made chemicals were damaging Earth's ozone layer.

MILDRED S. DRESSELHAUS
A physicist, engineer, and National Medal of Science winner, Dresselhaus has been a member of the Massachusetts Institute of Technology's electrical engineering faculty for more than thirty years.

NAM P. SUH
A professor of mechanical engineering at the Massachusetts Institute of Technology, Suh originated a branch of science called tribology, the study of how and why materials wear out.

OSCAR SUROS

As manager of engineering and architecture for the Port Authority of New York, this structural engineer is responsible for maintaining structures such as the George Washington Bridge and the World Trade Center.

LONNIE REID

A mechanical engineer, Reid headed NASA's Internal Fluid Mechanics Division. He also studied the flow of air through aircraft engines to develop quieter and cleaner equipment for passenger planes.

HAROLD ROSEN (left) and JOHN PIERCE (right)

These 1995 winners of the Charles Stark Draper Prize—the National Academy of Engineering's highest honor—designed, developed, and produced pioneering communications satellite networks in the 1960s. At Bell Laboratories, Pierce developed and published the first practical engineering calculations for space communication. After reading Pierce's work, Rosen worked at Hughes Aircraft to design a satellite communications system.

JACK S. KILBY (left) and ROBERT N. NOYCE (right)

In 1990 these engineers shared the Charles Stark Draper Prize for co-inventing the integrated circuit, better known as the semiconductor microchip. Their invention made miniaturization of computers possible and helped lead the world into the information age. Noyce's company provided integrated circuits to the space program for the onboard computer in the *Gemini* space capsule.

GRACE MURRAY HOPPER

While in the U.S. Navy WAVEs during World War II, Hopper developed operating programs for Mark I, an early computer. She wrote COBOL, the first English-language programming system.

MAE C. JEMISON

A chemical engineer, Jemison became the first African American woman in space in 1992. She also holds a doctorate in medicine from Cornell University. Today Jemison works as an educator.

JOHN B. SLAUGHTER

A specialist in electrical and environmental engineering, as well as physics, Slaughter has been a director of the National Science Foundation and is president of Occidental College.

MARY ROSS

A researcher in aerospace development and design concepts for interplanetary space travel, Native American Mary Ross, who is Cherokee, launched her career as a mathematician and teacher.

You Can Be an Engineer!

Do you ever wonder if the math and science you're learning at school is useful? Kids like Justin Cox, right, participating in a Young Technocrats engineering program in Washington, D.C., discover that math and science are a lot more than just solving equations on paper. For engineers, math and science are tools.

Engineers apply existing technology to real-world problems in new ways—or they invent new technologies that no one has thought of before. They begin with their imaginations and then use tools including math and science to make the dreams come true.

As Justin Cox discovered from his Young Technocrats experience, engineering often involves taking things apart and putting them back together in new ways. It's like putting a puzzle together. Does that idea get the gears in your brain turning? Then you're already thinking like an engineer.

"I always wondered, when I was growing up, *How does this doorknob work?* or thought, *Let me take this apart and see how it works,*" says NASA astronaut Jan Davis, a mechanical engineer. "If you're like that, engineering is right up your alley."

There are dozens of programs to help young people learn about the many branches of the engineering profession. To find out more about some of them, turn the page.

45

Other Sources of Information

PROFESSIONAL AND EDUCATIONAL ORGANIZATIONS:

American Association for the Advancement of Science
1333 H Street NW
Washington, DC 20005

The world's largest general science professional organization. Write for informational pamphlets and educational materials.

American Chemical Society
1155 16th Street NW
Washington, DC 20036

National membership organization of chemists of all kinds, including chemical engineers. Write for information about programs and publications for students.

American Institute of Aeronautics and Astronautics
Department JG
370 L'Enfant Promenade SW
Washington, DC 20024

Write for information about careers in aerospace engineering.

American Society for Engineering Education
1818 N Street NW, Suite #600
Washington, DC 20036

Organizes postdoctoral and faculty programs. Publishes Prism Magazine on Engineering.

American Society of Civil Engineers
Education Division
1801 Alexander Bell Drive
Reston, VA 20191-4400

Write for detailed information about youth programs and careers in civil engineering.

American Society of Mechanical Engineers
Education Department
345 East 47th Street
New York, NY 10017

Write for detailed information about careers in mechanical engineering.

Center for Children and Technology
Educational Development Corporation
96 Morton Street
New York, NY 10014

Write to receive the free Center for Children and Technology *Newsletter.*

Institute of Electrical and Electronics Engineers (IEEE)
345 East 47th Street
New York, NY 10017

Provides educational information about careers in electrical engineering, including jobs working with computers.

International Society for Technology in Education
1787 Agate Street
Eugene, OR 97403

Check out this organization's home page on the Internet at iste@oregon.uoregon.edu *for information about programs to bring technology into the classroom.*

Junior Engineering Technical Society (JETS)
1420 King Street, Suite 405
Alexandria, VA 22314-2715

A national organization dedicated to encouraging students to choose engineering as a career. Conducts academic programs and design competitions. Write for brochures, videotapes, and books.

National Aeronautics and Space Administration
Education Division
Code FEP
300 E Street NW
Washington, DC 20546-0001

Oversees the U.S. space program. Write for a wide variety of educational pamphlets and materials.

National Society of Black Engineers
Programs Division
1454 Duke Street
Alexandria, VA 22314

Offers information and a brochure on K–12 educational programs designed to encourage young African Americans to study math, science, and technology.

National Society of Professional Engineers

Education Foundation
1420 King Street
Alexandria, VA 22314-2715

The national membership organization for all engineering professionals. Write for educational pamphlets and materials.

Society of Hispanic Professional Engineers

5400 Olympic Blvd., Suite 306
Los Angeles, CA 90022

Promotes engineering opportunities for Hispanics. Publishes national newsletter, Hispanic Engineer magazine, and develops local outreach programs.

Society of Women Engineers

120 Wall Street
New York, NY 10005

A professional organization of women engineers. One of the group's goals is to encourage young women to study science and pursue careers in science and technology. Write for more information.

SPECIAL EVENTS:

National Engineers Week

P.O. Box 1020
Sewickley, PA 15143

Write for information about the annual week-long event in February that celebrates the work of engineers. National Engineers Week was founded in 1951 by the Society of Professional Engineers.

National Rube Goldberg™ Machine Contest

Purdue University
West Lafayette, IN 47907-1132

A fun, creative annual invention contest named for a cartoonist who drew incredibly complicated contraptions that performed simple tasks.

U.S. FIRST, The Competition

340 Commercial Street
Manchester, NH 03101

A national tournament that pits radio-controlled mechanical devices against each other in elimination matches. The acronym signifies For Inspiration and Recognition of Science and Technology.

MUSEUMS:

Boston Computer Museum

300 Congress Street
Boston, MA 02210

National Building Museum

401 F Street NW
Washington, DC 20001

National Air & Space Museum

Smithsonian Institution
Washington, DC 20560

For information about museums in your area, write to:

Association of Science Technology Centers

1025 Vermont Avenue NW
Suite 500
Washington, DC 20005

PHOTO CREDITS

Front cover: Mechanical engineer Erica Wittmann of The Boeing Company in Everett, Washington, inspects the hydraulic cables and backup emergency steering systems on a 777 jetliner. Hydraulic machinery, such as the wing flaps on an airplane, is operated by the movement of liquids. Photo by Steve Ringman

Back cover: Professor Bernard Y. Tao of the Agricultural and Biological Engineering Department at Purdue University does genetic research with plants to develop new, environmentally friendly industrial materials, foods, and pharmaceuticals. Photo by Paul Sancya

Page 1: Robotic arms with circuit board. Photo © Garry Gay/The Image Bank

Pages 2–3: Colorful fiber optics. Photo © Gregory Heisler/The Image Bank

Page 3: Engineer inspects jet engine used on commercial 747s and military aircraft. Photo by Chuck O'Rear/Westlight

Pages 4–5: San Francisco/Oakland Bay Bridge. Photo © 1997 Peter Menzel

Pages 6–7: © 1997 Bob Sacha

Page 8: (all) Barbara Ries

Page 9: (left) Paul Sancya; (center) Barbara Ries; (right) Nick Kelsh

Page 10: (top) Nick Kelsh; (bottom) © Kay Chernush/The Image Bank

Pages 10–11: NASA

Page 11: (top) © Dan Esgro/The Image Bank; (bottom) © 1997 Kim Steele

Pages 12–13: Photo-essay by J. Kyle Keener

Page 14: Stephanie Maze

Page 15: (top) Karen Kasmauski; (bottom left and right) Stephanie Maze

Page 16: (left and center) Stephanie Maze; (right) Paul Sancya

Page 17: (top) Cary Wolinsky; (bottom) Paul Sancya

Page 18: (top) Joanna Pinneo; (center) Annie Griffiths Belt; (bottom) © Rube Goldberg Inc./Courtesy of Purdue University

Page 19: (top) © William N. Fish/Courtesy of U.S. FIRST, The Competition; (bottom left) Paul Sancya; (bottom right) Stephanie Maze

Page 20: (top and center) © Adam Woolfitt/Woodfin Camp & Associates; (bottom left) Mercury Archives/Image Bank; (bottom right) Bettmann-Corbis

Page 21: (top left) © Hulton Deutsch Collection Limited/Woodfin Camp & Associates; (top right) Woodfin Camp & Associates; (second from top) The Bettmann Archive-Corbis; (second row from bottom, left and right) The Bettmann Archive-Corbis; (bottom) Mercury Archives/The Image Bank

Page 22: (top left) UPI/Bettmann-Corbis; (top center) Jodi Cobb/National Geographic Image Collection; (top right) Courtesy of *SWE Magazine*; (second row from top, left) Corbis-Bettmann; (second row from top, right) Mercury Archives/The Image Bank; (second from bottom) The Bettmann Archive-Corbis; (bottom) UPI/Bettmann-Corbis

Page 23: (top left) The Bettmann Archive-Corbis; (top center and right) UPI/Bettmann-Corbis; (center) © David W. Hamilton/The Image Bank; (center inset) Corbis-Bettmann; (bottom) UPI/Bettmann-Corbis

Page 24: (top row, left to right) Michael S. Yamashita; © Gregory Heisler/The Image Bank; NASA; © Paul Katz/The Image Bank; (center row, left to right) NASA; © Gregory Heisler/The Image Bank; © Guido Alberto Rossi/The Image Bank; Doug Wilson/Westlight; (bottom row, left to right) © Matthew Weinreb/The Image Bank; © The Stock Market/Ted Horowitz, 1997; © Joel Sartore

Page 25: (top row, left to right) © 1997 Richard T. Nowitz; © Catherine Karnow/Woodfin Camp & Associates; © Joe McNally; © Larry Keenan/The Image Bank; (second row from top, left to right) Steve Ringman; Peter Menzel; Robert Goodman/© National Geographic Image Collection; (second row from bottom, left to right) Roger Ressmeyer © 1997 Corbis; © The Stock Market/Brownie Harris, 1997;

© Michael S. Yamashita; (bottom row, left to right) © The Stock Market/Zefa/UK, 1997; © Chris Close/The Image Bank; © The Stock Market/Ted Horowitz, 1997

Pages 26–27: © Eric Meola/The Image Bank

Page 28: (top left) Chuck O'Rear/Woodfin Camp & Associates; (top right) Barbara Ries; (bottom left) Doug Menuez/SABA; (bottom right) © Weinberg-Clark/The Image Bank

Page 29: (top left) ©1997 Peter Essick-Aurora; (top right) ©1997 Jose Azel-Aurora; (center left) © Michael Rosenfeld/The Image Bank; (center right) Bill Tiernan; (bottom left) © William Edwards/The Image Bank; (bottom right) © Digital Art/Westlight

Page 30: (top) ©1997 Peter Essick-Aurora; (bottom) Seth Resnick © Liaison International

Page 31: (top) © Lou Jones/The Image Bank; (bottom left) © 1997 Peter Menzel; (bottom right) © 1997 Bob Sacha

Page 32 (top to bottom) © Mark Stephenson/Westlight; © Paul S. Howell/The Gamma Liaison Network; © 1997 Peter Menzel; © 1997 Peter Menzel

Page 33: (top) Robert Reichert/Liaison International; (bottom left) © 1997 Peter Menzel; (bottom right) © Lawrence Manning/Westlight

Page 34: (all) Lara Jo Regan

Page 35: Photos from the making of the movie *Jumanji* © 1995 TriStar Pictures Inc. Courtesy of TriStar Pictures Inc., and Industrial Light & Magic, a division of Lucas Digital Ltd. (top left) David Owen © 1995 Industrial Light & Magic, all rights reserved. Courtesy of Industrial Light & Magic, a division of Lucas Digital Ltd., and TriStar Pictures, Inc.; (right, top to bottom) Courtesy of TriStar Pictures Inc. and Industrial Light & Magic, a division of Lucas Digital Ltd.

Page 36: (top left) © Joel Sartore; (top right and bottom left) © 1997 Peter Menzel; (bottom right) © 1997 Richard T. Nowitz

Page 37: (top left) © Michael S. Yamashita; (top right) © 1997 Peter Menzel; (bottom left and right) © 1997 Peter Menzel

Page 38: (top left) © Melchior DiGiacomo/The Image Bank; (top right) © 1997 Richard T. Nowitz; (center right) © Webb Chappell/Courtesy of MIT Media Laboratory; (bottom right) Barbara Ries

Page 39: (top) © 1997 Richard T. Nowitz; (bottom left to right) Chuck O'Rear/Westlight; © 1997 Richard T. Nowitz; © Steve Dunwell/The Image Bank

Page 40: (top left) Stefano Cellai/Grazia Neri/Woodfin Camp & Associates

Pages 40–41: © Stephanie Maze

Page 41: (right, top to bottom) © 1997 Richard T. Nowitz; Raphael Gaillarde/Gamma Liaison; Raphael Gaillarde/Gamma Liaison; © Robb Kendrick-Aurora; (bottom left) © Xinhua/Gamma Liaison

Page 42: (top row, left to right) Courtesy of Historical American Engineering Record; © Hulton Deutsch Collection Limited/Woodfin Camp & Associates; Corbis-Bettmann; Courtesy of National Academy of Engineering; (bottom row, left to right) Courtesy of *SWE Magazine*; Courtesy of Occidental College, California; Courtesy of Massachusetts Institute of Technology; Courtesy of Massachusetts Institute of Technology

Page 43: (top left) Courtesy of *Hispanic Engineer* magazine; (top right) Courtesy of Lonnie Reid; (center row, left to right) Courtesy of the National Academy of Engineering; (bottom row, left to right) Courtesy of *SWE Magazine*; NASA; Courtesy of *Hispanic Engineer* magazine; Courtesy of *SWE Magazine*

Pages 44–45: Barbara Ries

Page 47: Gregory J. Harbaugh, aeronautical and astronautical engineer and STS-54 mission specialist aboard space shuttle *Endeavour*, waves to fellow crew members from the payload bay during a four-hour EVA (extravehicular activity) in space. Photo courtesy of NASA.

HQ CHILDRENS
764145
J 331.7 GRACE
Grace, Catherine O'Neill,
1950--
I want to be-- an engineer

I want to be-- an engineer /
J 620.0023 GRACE   764145

Grace, Catherine O'Neill,
WEST GEORGIA REGIONAL LIBRARY